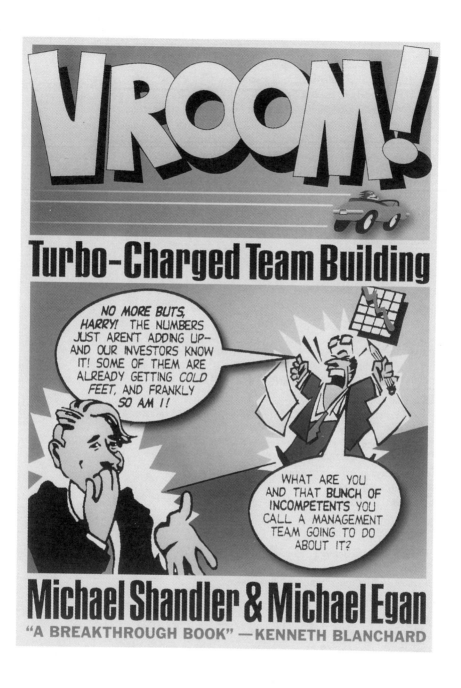

amacom

American Management Association

New York • Atlanta • Boston • Chicago • Kansas City • San Francisco • Washington, D. C.
Brussels • Mexico City • Tokyo • Toronto

This book is available at a special
discount when ordered in bulk quantities.
For information, contact Special Sales Department,
AMACOM, a division of American Management Association,
135 West 50th Street, New York, NY 10020.

This publication is designed to provide accurate and authoritative information in regard to the subject matter covered. It is sold with the
understanding that the publisher is not engaged in rendering legal,
accounting, or other professional service. If legal advice or other expert
assistance is required, the services of a competent professional person
should be sought.

Library of Congress Cataloging-in-Publication Data

Shandler, Michael
    Vroom! : turbo-charged team building / Michael Shandler & Michael
Egan.
      p. cm.
    ISBN 0-8144-7900-6
    1. Work groups.   I. Egan, Michael.   II. Title.
HD66.S484   1996
658.4'02—dc20   95-46216
                                                               CIP

Printing number

10 9 8 7 6 5 4 3 2 1

To our very patient wives and children—
and to our own team process,
from which we have learned more
than we can ever say

Foreword

Vroom! is a breakthrough book. It's fun, and easy to read, but packs a powerful message. *Vroom!* is about how to create inspired teamwork, and how to do it quickly. It presents a system that shows how outstanding products, services, and profits can be produced when people learn to work together as a team with a common purpose.

Although *Vroom!* is a comic, it presents leading-edge behavioral science in a brilliantly concise and "easy to get" form. As we follow Harry Black and his team in their discovery of new ways of working together, we learn that any group with a common purpose and an ethic of responsibility can become a truly high-performing team.

Vroom! is for those who see themselves as the primary agents of the changes we will have to make in business if we are to succeed in a global economy. *Vroom!* is a book for all those who are being challenged to transform their operating mode to include teamwork.

I recommend *Vroom!* to everyone who is interested in teamwork and wants the information in a fun and "easy to read" style.

Kenneth Blanchard, Ph.D.
Co-author, *The One Minute Manager* series

Preface

A comic book about team building? You must be joking!

Well, no, actually, though we hope *Vroom!* will make you laugh from time to time. We're the writing team of Michael Shandler and Michael Egan, with a big message to pass on. It's this: Teams are the core units of the future for American (and world) companies, and the foundation work of building them successfully can be accomplished relatively quickly. That's why we've subtitled our book *Turbo-Charged Team Building*. If the principles and processes described in the story are applied, any group can transform itself at warp speed into a high-performing team.

We know that's a big claim, which is one reason we chose to express it in picture form. Seeing is believing. Organizations are complex things made up of systems, structures, processes, and people—whole "cultures." These are the context for often complex interactions between individuals, departments, or functions, interactions that powerfully influence the destiny of organizations, yet are not easily depicted in the slippery abstractions of language.

But—as they say—a picture's worth a thousand verbal hooks. Illustrations also help to present and clarify notions, concepts, and theories in action, which can be difficult to master with words alone. That's why we've caught our ideas for you in the comic book medium.

And here's the biggest joke of all: Neither of us can draw! So how did we do it? The answer is, of course, by computer. All the pictures and images in *Vroom!* were generated using a draw program and clip art. We would like here to acknowledge specifically the flexibility and ingenuity of software provided by New Vision Technologies.

Vroom! Turbo-Charged Team Building is a self-help business book in graphic form—a serious but amusing tale, rendered vividly (we hope) in words and images. Our intended readers are businesspeople at every level, from company presidents and CEOs to middle managers, union leaders, and rank-and-file workers interested in how groups function and how their performance is maximized.

The narrative tells of Harry Black and his R&D team at ElectroMotion, Inc., a subsidiary of U.S. Energy Corporation. USECO, a giant car-and-truck battery manufacturer, has given Harry and his colleagues the mission of creating a revolutionary new technology—a "super battery" capable of powering an E.V. (electric vehicle) at least 500 miles between recharges.

At the time we take up the story, Harry's project is stalled. He is summoned to a meeting with company president and CEO, J. D. "Tommy" Gunn, who tells him in no uncertain terms to get his project back on track—or lose his job. J. D. gives Harry and his management team less than a year to refashion themselves and their division into a force capable of designing and developing the elusive super battery. How Harry does this is the substance of the action.

At the conclusion of each chapter, a one-page summary of the main ideas is presented. We call these reviews "Under the Hood With Harry." The book ends with a big "Under the Hood," listing and referencing the key concepts employed—a sort of graphic index.

There's a subplot associated with the tale. Harry's marriage, like his career, is at crisis point. His wife, Jenny, an author, feels that she is having to sacrifice her ambitions for her husband's. Gradually Harry comes to realize that many of the skills and concepts that he has learned from building his management team can also help with his marriage, and in a final meeting he and Jenny sit down together and work things out.

Well, what would a comic book be without a happy ending? Besides, we believe in the ideas presented, and know, on the basis of more than twenty years' experience, that they can and do work.

We hope you enjoy *Vroom!* as much as we've enjoyed designing and presenting it to you.

Michael Shandler
Michael Egan
Amherst, Mass.

Acknowledgments

Our editors at AMACOM, Adrienne Hickey, Mike Sivilli, and Jacquie Flynn, did a terrific job, and we'd like to acknowledge their contribution. Andrew Rock, our agent, was enthusiastic about *Vroom!* from the outset, and played a key role.

The following friends and colleagues gave us feedback, comments, and ideas as *Vroom!* evolved, and we'd like to thank them: Mary and Herb Bernstein, Martin Bock, Rob Brandt, Kendra Crossen, Jack Curtis, Ellen Grobman, Alan Hurwitz, Bill Lowry, Laurie Pearlman, Paul Roud, Manju Shandler, Nina Shandler, Sara Shandler, John Simmons, and Ervin Staub.

Michael Shandler personally acknowledges Michael Egan, my co-author, for his conception of *Vroom!* as a computer-generated comic book, for his innovation, and for his devotion to the project through its many phases. I'm grateful to Charlie Kiefer, chairman of Innovation Associates, for introducing me to visionary planning and team-building, an approach that has greatly influenced my work. My former colleagues at Innovation Associates, Joel Yanowitz, Sherry Immediato, and Peter Senge, contributed significantly to my understanding of high-performing organizations. I'm also grateful to Martin Rutte, president of Livelihood, Inc., who introduced me to the concept of 100 Percent Responsibility, a premise that has significantly shaped my personal and professional work. My thanks to Jack Rosenblum and his colleagues at The Atlanta Consulting Group for the concept of Managing by Agreement, and for the many ways in which they have furthered my organizational and interpersonal understanding. My thanks to Dick Heiman and the Campbell Group for providing a ten-year proving ground for many of the concepts in the book.

Michael Egan personally thanks Jim Freeman and Ernie Gallo for timely comments. To the many trainers and managers with whom I've worked in recent years, thanks also. But most of all, I would like to thank Michael Shandler, my co-author, for his energy, commitment, and unfailing help.

M.S.
M.E.E.

CHAPTER ONE
HARRY GETS A SHOCK!

-2-

AND THIS IS **DON BASKIN**, DIRECTOR OF PURCHASING. A LITTLE ECCENTRIC, BUT HE KNOWS ALL THE NUMBERS --AND **UNDERSTANDS** THEM, TOO!

LAST BUT NOT LEAST, **SALLY JONES**, CHIEF ENGINEER. THE **CANNIEST** CORPORATE POLITICIAN I KNOW, I'M GLAD SHE'S ON **MY SIDE**... *NOW.* SHE WASN'T ALWAYS!

SALLY, DON, TONY AND WANDA ARE MY **DIRECT REPORTS!** AFTER THEM COME A SMALL GROUP OF **MIDDLE MANAGERS**--OVERALL, A BUNCH OF THE **NICEST**, **HARDWORKINGEST** PEOPLE ANYONE COULD ASK FOR!

THINGS **WEREN'T** ALWAYS **THAT GOOD** AROUND HERE! IN FACT, JUST ABOUT **A YEAR AGO** WE CAME CLOSER THAN A G.I.'S HAIRCUT TO **SHUTTING DOWN**--AND TAKING THE REST OF USECO WITH US!

IN MARCH, **GENERAL MOTORS** SUDDENLY ANNOUNCED PLANS TO **MARKET-TEST** ITS OWN ELECTRIC VEHICLE CALLED THE *IMPACT!* SOON AFTERWARDS **ALAN COCCINI**, *THE* WORLD AUTHORITY, DECLARED THAT **ONLY 'HYBRID'** GAS-ELECTRIC CARS WERE **PRACTICAL!**

G.M. MARKETS IMPACT

HARUMPH! COME INTO MY **OFFICE, HARRY,** AND **SHUT** THE DOOR!

THELMA, HOLD MY CALLS!

THE NEXT DAY I WAS ABRUPTLY **SUMMONED** TO AN URGENT MEETING WITH USECO'S **CEO** AND **CHAIRMAN** OF THE BOARD, J.D. 'TOMMY' GUNN.

HE ARRIVED LATE, CARRYING A **BIG** REPORT. HE DID NOT SEEM **TOO** PLEASED TO SEE ME!

SUDDENLY J.D. SOFTENED...

HARRY, MY BOY, I'M **NOT** EXAGGERATING. THE **FUTURE OF USECO ITSELF** IS AT STAKE! FRANKLY, WE'RE **BETTING EVERYTHING** ON THE **ELMO!**

PULL THIS OFF, AND WE'LL ALL BE **VERY** GRATEFUL!

GET MY DRIFT??

I GOT HIS **DRIFT**, ALL RIGHT--INCLUDING THE PART THAT MIGHT **DRIFT ME** RIGHT **OUT OF MY JOB!**

WANDA? TONY? NAH, I BET IT'S SALLY JONES!

HEADING BACK TO MY OFFICE, I WONDERED WHO WAS REPORTING TO J.D. ABOUT ME, AND FELT STUNG BY HIS INSINUATION THAT I'D LET DOWN **JOE WISE**, MY FIRST BOSS AND MENTOR!

JOE REALLY **HAD** GONE OUT ON A **LIMB** TO GET ME THE PLUM JOB AT ELECTROMOTION! HE WAS **WIDELY RESPECTED** AS A LEADER AND **ORGANIZATIONAL GENIUS** WHO'D BUILT HIS ENGINEERING COMPANY FROM **NOTHING** TO **DOMINANCE** IN JUST **THREE YEARS!**

JOSEPH WISE
PRESIDENT

THE LAST I'D HEARD, HE WAS IN WASHINGTON, ADVISING THE GOVERNMENT ON INDUSTRIAL POLICY!

WHAT WOULD JOE SAY AT A TIME LIKE THIS?

HARRY, INSANITY IS DOING THE SAME THING AND EXPECTING A DIFFERENT RESULT! YOU'LL HAVE TO CHANGE!

SUDDENLY I KNEW WHERE TO GET THE HELP I SO DESPERATELY NEEDED!

YEAH! JOE WISE!

CHAPTER TWO
HARRY WISES UP

...SALLY SPOKE UP.

WELL, HARRY, YOU'RE **IN CHARGE!** I RECKON THE **INITIATIVE** SHOULD COME FROM **YOU!**

YOU'RE **RIGHT,** SALLY! LET ME GIVE THIS SOME **MORE THOUGHT,** AND I'LL GET **BACK** TO YOU!

AS SOON AS THEY WERE GONE, I PUT A CALL THROUGH TO MY OLD BOSS, **JOE WISE,** AND WE HAD A LONG CHAT. I TOLD HIM I **HAD** TO GET MY OPERATION TOGETHER *FAST!*

HEY, HARRY! HOW'RE YOU DOING?

NOT GOOD, JOE! **BIG** TROUBLE... ROUGH INTERVIEW WITH **J.D.**...GOT TO SHOW SOME **REAL PROGRESS** IN TIME FOR NEXT YEAR'S STOCK-HOLDERS' MEETING... *HELP!!*

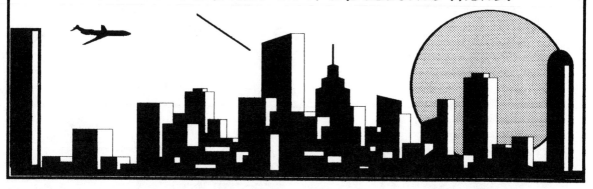

JOE ASKED ME A LOT OF **DETAILED QUESTIONS** ABOUT MY UNIT AND WHY TOMMY GUNN HAD **SHOT ME DOWN.** FINALLY HE SAID:

HARRY, YOUR **KEY PEOPLE** ARE ALL OVER THE **MAP!** THERE'S **COMPETITION** FOR RESOURCES, **DISAGREEMENT** ABOUT TECHNOLOGY AND EVEN ABOUT YOUR **BASIC OBJECTIVES!** ARE YOU DEVELOPING A **BATTERY** OR A **GAS-ELECTRIC HYBRID?**

WELL, I... THAT IS...

EXACTLY, HARRY! J.D.'S **QUITE RIGHT!** YOU'VE GOT TO GET YOUR **ENTIRE MANAGEMENT TEAM** IN **SYNCH**—FIRST ABOUT **WHERE** YOU THINK YOU'RE ALL **GOING,** THEN ABOUT THE BEST WAY TO **GET THERE!**

GOOD, HARRY! THEN I'LL BE GLAD TO **HELP**! SO LET'S START WITH YOU: WHAT'S YOUR **MAIN DESIRED RESULT** FROM THIS PROCESS?

THAT'S AN **EASY ONE**, JOE! BY YEAR'S END, THE *ELMO* **REGAINS** ITS STATUS AS THE **LEADING PROTOTYPE** ELECTRIC CAR!

OKAY, HARRY, LET'S CALL THAT YOUR **VISION**--YOUR **PERSONAL VISION**. NOW TELL ME: WHO IS GOING TO **MAKE IT HAPPEN**?

WELL, I **SUPPOSE** IN THE END **WE ALL ARE**, EVERYONE WORKING HERE AT ELECTRO-MOTION!

RIGHT?

HARRY, IN **BUSINESS** THERE ARE **THREE** KINDS OF **PEOPLE**: THOSE WHO **LET** THINGS HAPPEN, THOSE WHO **HELP** THINGS HAPPEN AND THOSE WHO **MAKE** THINGS HAPPEN! NOW **WHO'S** RESPONSIBLE FOR REALIZING **YOUR** VISION?

I GUESS IF YOU PUT IT **THAT** WAY, JOE, I AM! BUT I CAN'T DO IT **ALONE**!

IT WAS A COUPLE OF SUPERVISORS FROM THE SWING SHIFT, WANTING ME TO SETTLE A DISPUTE ABOUT **WHOSE JOB** IT WAS TO DELIVER SOME PARTS! I JUST LISTENED FOR A WHILE AS THEY **WENT AT IT**, THEN TOLD THE SENIOR MAN IT WAS *HIS* RESPONSIBILITY. THEY **BARGED OUT** AGAIN, STILL ARGUING.

BLAME... JUSTIFICATION... RECRIMINATION... *NOT* A *TEAM!*

HONK!

HONK!

I HAVE A **LOT OF FAITH** IN JOE, BUT HOW CAN **ANY** SYSTEM GET GUYS LIKE **THOSE** TO WORK TOGETHER?

THE **TRAFFIC** OUT OF THE CITY THAT EVENING WAS **HORRENDOUS**, SO UNLUCKILY I GOT BACK **HOME** EVEN *LATER* THAN USUAL!

I REALIZED THERE WAS **TROUBLE** WHEN I FOUND THE HOUSE COLD, DARK AND EMPTY...

...AND A **NOTE** FROM MY **WIFE** TAPED TO THE FRIDGE!

Harry, where the hell are you? I have a career too, you know! Kids are with Lisa. You and I need to talk--soon.

Jenny

THEN I REMEMBERED I'D **PROMISED** TO BE HOME IN TIME SO THAT JENNY, A **WRITER,** COULD HAVE DINNER WITH HER **EDITOR!** IN THE HEAT OF THE DAY IT HAD ALL **COMPLETELY** SLIPPED MY MIND!

JENNY WAS A **WONDERFUL WIFE** AND **MOTHER,** BUT FOR THE PAST SIX MONTHS OUR **SCHEDULES** HAD BEEN IN **MAJOR** CONFLICT! *IT LOOKED AS IF THE CRISIS IN MY MARRIAGE WAS FINALLY COMING TO A HEAD!*

UNDER THE HOOD WITH HARRY

WORKING PREMISES

PERIODICALLY, JOE WISE POINTS OUT TO HARRY THAT CERTAIN ATTITUDES HELD BY HARRY INHIBIT DESIRED RESULTS. FOR EXAMPLE, THE ATTITUDE OF "I'LL LET IT HAPPEN" IS LESS LIKELY TO LEAD TO DESIRED OUTCOMES THAN THE STANCE "I'LL MAKE IT HAPPEN."

THESE PROACTIVE PSYCHOLOGICAL SHIFTS PROPOSED IN _VROOM!_ ARE CALLED WORKING PREMISES.

WORKING PREMISES HAVE A BIAS FOR ACTION AND ARE SOLUTION AND RESULT-ORIENTED, REINFORCING THE PREMISE AND SETTING IN MOTION A POSITIVE CYCLE.

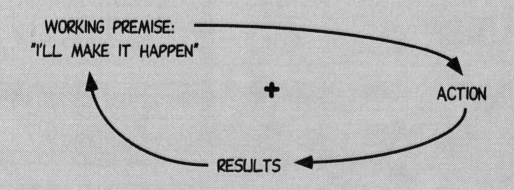

WORKING PREMISE:
"I'LL MAKE IT HAPPEN"

+

ACTION

RESULTS

CHAPTER THREE
THINGS GET HOTTER!

I RECEIVED JOE'S MATERIALS THE NEXT DAY--TWO BOOKS ON **LEADERSHIP** AND THE DRAFT OF A **LONG ARTICLE** ON **TURBO-CHARGED TEAM BUILDING** HE'D WRITTEN **HIMSELF!**

IT TOOK ME A **WEEK** TO READ IT ALL, THINKING AND MAKING NOTES. WHAT I LEARNED CHANGED MY ENTIRE **PHILOSOPHY OF MANAGEMENT**--AND LIFE!

THERE WERE **TWO KEYS** TO JOE'S *TCTB* SYSTEM-- THE POWER OF PURPOSE AND WHAT HE CALLED ONE HUNDRED PERCENT RESPONSIBILITY.

ONE HUNDRED PER-CENT RESPONSIBILITY MEANS JUST WHAT IT SAYS--THAT WE EACH AGREE TO ACCEPT *TOTAL RESPONSIBILITY* FOR OUR LIVES! OUR *TRIUMPHS* ARE OUR OWN, BUT SO TOO ARE OUR *DEFEATS!*

WHEN WE **BLAME** CIRCUMSTANCES OR OTHER PEOPLE FOR OUR **DIFFICULTIES**, WE GIVE THEM **CONTROL** OVER US, BECAUSE UNLESS *THEY* CHANGE OR ACT, WE'RE **POWERLESS!**

SURE, IN **REAL LIFE,** PEOPLE AND SITUATIONS OFTEN *DO* CREATE **PROBLEMS** FOR US...

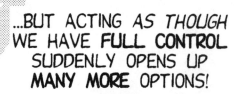

...BUT ACTING *AS THOUGH* WE HAVE **FULL CONTROL** SUDDENLY OPENS UP **MANY MORE** OPTIONS!

I FOUND THE IDEA INCREDIBLY EM-POWERING! IT MEANT THAT **NOBODY BUT I** WAS **MASTER** OF MY **FATE!** BY ACTING, I COULD **CHANGE** THINGS!

I THEN AND THERE REALIZED THAT IT WAS 100 **PERCENT UP TO ME** TO SAVE BOTH ELECTROMOTION **AND MY MARRIAGE!** FOR THE FIRST TIME SINCE THE DAY TOMMY GUNN BLEW HIS STACK, I FELT **GOOD!**

JOE'S OTHER BIG IDEA, AS I SAID, WAS CALLED "THE POWER OF PURPOSE."

IT TOOK ME A WHILE TO FULLY APPRECIATE THE WISDOM OF THIS, BUT THEN ONE DAY I READ A REPORT ABOUT NELSON MANDELA AND THE AFRICAN NATIONAL CONGRESS...

..AN ORGANIZATION SUSTAINED SINCE 1912 BY ITS VISION OF DEMOCRATIC CHANGE IN SOUTH AFRICA! WHEN MANDELA WAS ELECTED PRESIDENT IN 1994, THE DREAM WAS FULFILLED!

LATER I HEARD ABOUT TERRY FOX, THE ONE-LEGGED MAN WHO HAD THE WILL TO RUN 3000 MILES ACROSS CANADA.

CLAP! CLAP!

YAY!

AND I REALIZED THAT IF I COULD GET EVERYONE AT ELECTROMOTION PULLING IN THE SAME DIRECTION---WITH THE SAME SENSE OF PURPOSE AS TERRY FOX, MANDELA AND THE A.N.C.---WE'D BE UNSTOPPABLE!

I CALLED JOE AGAIN, AS AGREED, AND TOGETHER WE PLANNED A **THREE-DAY, OFF-SITE MEETING** FOR THE FULL MANAGEMENT TEAM.

EACH DAY HAS ITS *TASK*, HARRY! ON THE FIRST, YOU WORK OUT YOUR *VISION*. *DAY TWO*, YOU DESIGN THE *RIGHT PROCESS* TO ACHIEVE IT! THE *FINAL DAY*, YOU DECIDE HOW TO ENROLL THE *REST* OF ELECTROMOTION!

JOE ADDED THAT WE SHOULD GO **SOMEWHERE NICE**, SO THAT PEOPLE COULD **RELAX** BETWEEN **SESSIONS**.

I PREPARED THE DETAILS CAREFULLY AND, AS A FINAL FLOURISH, DECIDED TO MEET AT A HOTEL IN FLORIDA.

THEN I MEMO'D ALL MY MANAGERS! EVERYONE WAS **HAPPY**! LITTLE DID THEY KNOW WHAT JOE AND I HAD IN MIND FOR THEM!

TING!
TING!

THEN, AFTER COFFEE, I CALLED THEIR ATTENTION AND GOT TO MY FEET.

FRIENDS AND COLLEAGUES, **THANK YOU** ALL FOR MAKING THE EFFORT TO BE HERE!

I **REALIZE**, OF COURSE, JUST HOW **TOUGH** IT WAS FOR YOU TO **LEAVE WORK** AND COME TO **SUNNY FLORIDA!**

JUST AS LONG AS **YOU'RE PAYING** FOR IT, HARRY!

HA! HA!

HA! HA! HA!

HA! HA!

THAT'S OKAY. YOU FOLKS **KNOW** I ALWAYS GET VALUE FOR MY MONEY!

YEAH, YOU'RE **PRETTY** TIGHT, HARRY!

HA! HA!

ACTUALLY, I'M QUITE **SERIOUS!** THIS MAY **LOOK** LIKE A **VACATION** TO YOU, BUT IN FACT YOU ARE GOING TO **WORK HARDER** THAN YOU'VE EVER WORKED IN YOUR LIFE!

"JUST THE OTHER DAY, TWO OF OUR **BEST PEOPLE** CAME TO SEE ME BECAUSE THEY COULDN'T DECIDE **WHOSE JOB** IT WAS TO CARRY OUT A ROUTINE TASK! WE LOST *TIME, ENERGY AND MONEY!* SUPPOSE EACH HAD JUST TAKEN THE **SIMPLE RESPONSIBILITY** TO DO IT, FOR ELECTROMOTION'S SAKE?"

SOMEHOW WE'VE BUILT A **CULTURE OF BLAME,** C.Y.A. BEHAVIORS, AND **MISTRUST!** IN THE NEXT **THREE DAYS** WE'RE GOING TO *HAVE* TO **CHANGE** ALL THAT, STARTING WITH **OURSELVES!**

YOU'RE **ABSOLUTELY RIGHT** ABOUT OUR **CULTURE,** HARRY. BUT **REALLY CHANGING** IT IMPLIES...

...A **VERY DIFFERENT** WAY OF DOING THINGS!

EXACTLY, JACK! OUR OLD MODEL JUST DOESN'T **WORK ANYMORE!** *WE NEED TO COME TOGETHER AS A* **TEAM,** *WITH EACH OF US TAKING FULL* **RESPONSIBILITY** *FOR THE SUCCESS OF ALL!*

UNDER THE HOOD WITH HARRY

THE 100 PERCENT RESPONSIBILITY CYCLE

100 PERCENT RESPONSIBILITY = FOCUS ON DESIRED RESULTS
= POWER FOR POSITIVE ACTION
= EXPANDED OPTIONS
= NO EXCUSES AND NO BLAME WHEN THINGS GO WRONG

WHEN A CRITICAL MASS ADOPTS 100 PERCENT RESPONSIBILITY,
THIS FORCE CREATES ORGANIZATIONAL EMPOWERMENT,
WHICH AFFECTS RESULTS, IMPROVES MORALE, AND
REINFORCES THE CYCLE.

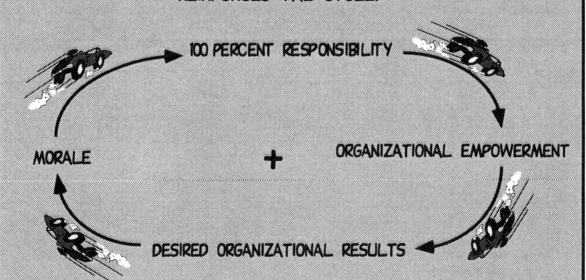

CHAPTER FOUR
ACTION-PLUS MEETINGS

EVEN THOUGH I THINK JENNY'S *WRONG*, I'M *ONE HUNDRED PERCENT* RESPONSIBLE FOR MY MARRIAGE!

AFTER DINNER THAT EVENING, I WENT FOR A **LONG STROLL** ALONG THE BEACH. I WAS *HAUNTED* BY MY **OWN WORDS**.

WE'D HAD A **HUGE ROW** JUST BEFORE I LEFT FOR **FLORIDA**--I WAS **MISSING** HER NIECE'S WEDDING!

FINE, HARRY! JUST DON'T BE *SURPRISED* IF I'M *NOT HERE* WHEN YOU GET **BACK**!

SKREEK!

HARRY, YOU PROMISED ME **SIX MONTHS** AGO YOU'D COME!

DAMMIT, JENNY, I *HAVE TO GO* TO THIS MEETING!

"WHAT TO DO WHEN SOMEONE FALLS..."

"...AND HOW TO **TRUST** ONE ANOTHER SO THAT WE ALL MAKE THE CLIMB SAFELY!"

"FINALLY, WE'LL ESTABLISH SOME **GROUND RULES** FOR OUR **FUTURE WORK TOGETHER** AND MAKE A **PLAN** FOR BRINGING THESE IDEAS TO THE **REST** OF **ELECTROMOTION.** *ARE YOU WITH ME?*"

YEAH, WE'RE WITH YOU, HARRY!

WHAT'S THE FIRST STEP?

BASIC MOUNTAIN-EERING! WE HAVE TO LEARN HOW TO CLIMB TOGETHER AS A *TEAM!*

"RIGHT NOW, WE'RE NOT A TRUE TEAM. WE'RE MOSTLY CLIMBING THE LADDER OF SUCCESS AS INDIVIDUALS."

"THAT'S SHORT-TERM THINKING! IT'S NOT HARD TO SEE WHERE IT LEADS TO!"

WHAT WE'RE LACKING IS THE SYNERGY OF TEAMWORK! TO SURVIVE, WE MUST BECOME MORE THAN JUST AN AGGREGATE OF TALENTED INDIVIDUALS!

SYNERGY IS GROUP ENERGY MULTIPLIED BY ITSELF! NOTE HERE THAT IT'S THE FUNCTION *BETWEEN* THE NUMBERS THAT MAKES THE DIFFERENCE!

THE MATH OF SYNERGY

$$3 - 3 = 0$$
$$3 \div 3 = 1$$
$$3 + 3 = 6$$
$$3 \times 3 = 9!$$

"EFFECTIVE CORPORATE MOUNTAINEERING TODAY TAKES *REAL* TEAMWORK! WE'RE ALL CONNECTED BY AN INVISIBLE CORD! WE'LL MAKE IT TOGETHER--OR NOT AT ALL!"

AND FOR US, ACHIEVING THE SYNERGY OF TEAMWORK MEANS, FIRST, LEARNING TO MANAGE OUR MEETINGS BETTER--AS A TEAM!

BECAUSE LET'S FACE IT...

"MOST OF OUR MEETINGS WASTE TIME AND RARELY ACHIEVE RESULTS! THAT'S NOT TEAMWORK, FOLKS!"

ONE OF THE BIG IDEAS I'D GOT FROM JOE WAS THAT IN ORGANIZATIONS, MEETINGS ARE THE HEART OF TEAMWORK. HE'D DEVELOPED A SYSTEM CALLED ACTION-PLUS MEETING MANAGEMENT!

HARRY, A GREAT TEAM BUILDS ITS SOLIDARITY IN ACTION! IT GETS RESULTS BY BRINGING PEOPLE TOGETHER! ACTION-PLUS SHOWS THEM HOW TO FOCUS ON BOTH THE OUTCOMES THEY WANT AND COOPERATIVE WAYS TO GET THERE!

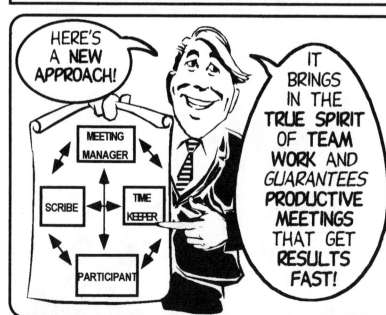

HERE'S A NEW APPROACH!

MEETING MANAGER

SCRIBE

TIME KEEPER

PARTICIPANT

IT BRINGS IN THE TRUE SPIRIT OF TEAMWORK AND GUARANTEES PRODUCTIVE MEETINGS THAT GET RESULTS FAST!

I INTRODUCED MY GROUP TO JOE'S ACTION-PLUS SYSTEM. IN THE NEXT FEW DAYS WE WOULD BE GOING THROUGH A SERIES OF TEAM-BUILDING MEETINGS!

"UNDER THIS NEW SYSTEM, WE USE TIME MORE EFFICIENTLY, WORK TOWARD AN AGREED RESULT, AND TAKE CARE THAT EVERYONE'S VOICE IS HEARD. DECISIONS ARE MADE BY CONSENSUS!"

JOE HAD WARNED ME THERE MIGHT BE SOME EARLY RESISTANCE. AS USUAL, HE WAS RIGHT!

YEAH, MAJORITY RULE!

HARRY, I'M ALL FOR TEAMWORK, BUT I DON'T UNDERSTAND ALL THIS TALK ABOUT CONSENSUS! WHY CAN'T WE JUST VOTE?

I TAKE YOUR POINT, DAN. YOURS TOO, MYRNA. THE TROUBLE WITH VOTING IS NOT THAT THE MAJORITY WINS, BUT THAT A MINORITY LOSES! WE NEED A WAY OF ARRIVING AT DECISIONS THAT UNITES US AS A TEAM, NOT ONE THAT DIVIDES US INTO FACTIONS!

"BUILDING CONSENSUS *IS* THE TEAMWORK PROCESS! **ALL VIEWS** ARE **HEARD** AND **RESPECTED**. WE PLAY **WIN-WIN** WITH EACH OTHER UNTIL FINALLY WE'RE **ALIGNED**, WHICH MEANS EVERYONE MUST FEEL AT LEAST ABLE TO *SUPPORT* THE OUTCOME."

I DUNNO, HARRY...

WHAT IF SOMEONE **DISAGREES STRONGLY ENOUGH** TO REALLY FIGHT?

THAT'S WHERE THE **TEAMWORK** COMES IN, DAN! WE **WORK OUT** OUR DIFFERENCES IN A **WIN-WIN** SPIRIT. AFTER THE MEETING, WE **SELF-EVALUATE** AND MAKE **CORRECTIONS**!

DAN, ISN'T IT **TRUE** THAT MOST OF OUR MEETINGS **DO WASTE TIME?**

LET'S GIVE HARRY'S IDEAS A TRY!

YEAH, OKAY, **WANDA!** HOW DOES IT **WORK, HARRY?**

UNDER THE HOOD WITH HARRY

MEETING MANAGEMENT

1. CHOOSE A MEETING MANAGER, SCRIBE AND TIME KEEPER.

2. AGREE ON DESIRED RESULTS OF MEETING.

3. AGREE ON A PROCESS FOR ACHIEVING THE DESIRED RESULTS AND A TIME FOR EACH STEP IN THE PROCESS.

4. STAY ON ONE TOPIC AT A TIME.

5. WHEN UNRELATED, BUT IMPORTANT, POINTS ARISE, PLACE THEM IN A "BIN" FOR LATER REFERENCE.

6. HEAR FROM EVERYONE. KEEP AN OPEN MIND. FOCUS ON DESIRED RESULTS.

7. USE TIME CONSCIOUSLY. EXTEND TIME WHERE NECESSARY TO ACHIEVE DESIRED RESULTS.

8. DON'T RAILROAD DECISIONS. PLAY WIN-WIN.

9. KEEP A VISIBLE RECORD OF GROUP AGREEMENTS, PREFERABLY ON A FLIP CHART.

10. WHEN YOU ARE FINISHED, EVALUATE THE MEETING TO LEARN HOW YOU CAN IMPROVE NEXT TIME.

CHAPTER FIVE
THE VISION

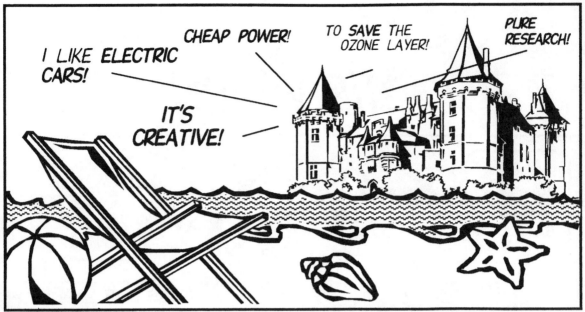

ELECTROMOTION **ALSO** NEEDS A **HUMAN VISION**--A **COLLECTIVE PURPOSE** THAT'S **BROADER, WIDER** AND **DEEPER** THAN JUST TURNING A PROFIT—EVEN THOUGH WE MUST HAVE THAT **TOO!**

NO **PROFIT**, NO **ELECTRO-MOTION!**

BUT **NO VISION** *ALSO* MEANS **NO ELECTRO-MOTION!** "WHERE THERE'S **NO VISION**, THE PEOPLE **PERISH**," AS THE BIBLE SAYS!

WHERE ARE WE **GOING? WHY?**

HOW WILL WE KNOW WHEN WE **GET THERE?**

AND, **MONEY ASIDE**, WHAT DO WE **WANT** FOR OUR **EFFORT?**

HARRY, YOU'RE VERY **ELOQUENT**, BUT I'M STILL NOT FULLY **CLEAR** ABOUT WHAT YOU MEAN! COULD YOU GIVE SOME **EXAMPLES?**

"SURE, DEIRDRE! I THINK ONE OF THE **MOST INSPIRING VISIONS** OF OUR TIME WAS JOHN KENNEDY'S **CALL** TO PUT A MAN ON THE MOON BY THE END OF THE **SIXTIES!**"

"ANOTHER ONE WAS MARTIN LUTHER KING'S *'I HAVE A DREAM'* SPEECH! **MILLIONS** OF PEOPLE WERE MOVED!"

"WE NEED TO SET OURSELVES THE SAME KIND OF **AUDACIOUS GOALS**! A GREAT VISION IS A **STRETCH**— BUT AN **ACHIEVABLE ONE!**"

VISION-EERING

HARRY, I THINK I JUST GOT YOUR **POINT**! A *POWERFUL VISION* IS LIKE THE **BATTERY** THAT WILL SOMEDAY **DRIVE** THE *ELMO!* IT'S THE **DYNAMO** THAT MAKES US **VROOM!**

"YOU'RE **RIGHT**, TONY! WITHOUT A **VISION**, WE'RE JUST A **BUNCH** OF **UNCONNECTED PARTS!**"

"BUT **POWERED** BY A VISION, WE CAN **BLAST OFF** INTO THE TWENTY-FIRST CENTURY!"

VROOM!

MYRNA AGREED TO BE **MEETING MANAGER**, TONY MILLS **SCRIBE** AND JACK SMITS **TIMEKEEPER**. THE GROUP CHOSE **OPEN DISCUSSION** AS ITS PROCESS. WE BEGAN BY GENERATING A SERIES OF **HARD QUESTIONS** ABOUT **OURSELVES**, OUR **CORE VALUES**, AND EVEN OUR **HOPES** AND **DREAMS!**

* WHAT DO I REALLY CARE ABOUT?

* WHAT DO I WANT TO CREATE/ACCOMPLISH?

* WHAT DO I WANT THE HALLMARKS OF OUR PRODUCT TO BE?

* WHAT CONTRIBUTIONS WILL OUR PRODUCT MAKE?

* HOW DO I WANT TO FEEL IN THIS ORGANIZATION?

* WHAT VALUES ARE IMPORTANT TO ME?

* HOW DO I WANT US TO TREAT ONE ANOTHER?

* AM I CLEAR ABOUT WHAT BUSINESS WE'RE IN?

* WHO ARE OUR STAKEHOLDERS?

* CAN I CREATE A WIN-WIN?

THE ROOM FELL **SILENT** AS PEOPLE THOUGHT LONG AND DEEP. IT WAS AN EXERCISE IN **CONCENTRATION** AND **SINCERITY**.

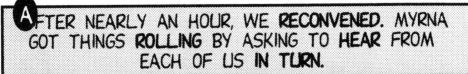

SYNERGY AND TEAMWORK!

WE'RE A TEAM OF PROFESSIONALS!

CUSTOMERS FIRST!

WIN-WIN!

FAIRNESS AND INTEGRITY

NON-POLLUTING ENERGY!

CUTTING-EDGE TECHNOLOGY!

A FEW **THEMES** QUICKLY EMERGED, BUT THEN SALLY JONES, OUR **CHIEF ENGINEER**, SAID SOMETHING THAT TURNED OUT TO BE **MOMENTOUS** IN ITS **IMPLICATIONS**!

HARRY, I THINK IT'S **GREAT** THAT WE'RE GETTING CLEAR ABOUT OUR **GENERAL DIRECTION**, BUT THERE'S A MORE **FUNDAMENTAL QUESTION** WE MUST SETTLE FIRST! ARE WE BUILDING A **BATTERY** OR A **GAS-ELECTRIC HYBRID** CAR??

FOR SOME TIME NOW WE'VE FELT IN ENGINEERING THAT WE COULD DEVELOP THE ELMO **SUPER** BATTERY...

BUT FRANKLY, **YOUR WAVERING** AROUND THE ISSUE HAS BEEN A **MAJOR** OBSTACLE!

SHE'S QUITE RIGHT, HARRY!

HOW CAN WE FOLLOW WHEN WE DON'T KNOW WHERE YOU'RE GOING?

FOR A WHILE I **DIDN'T KNOW** WHAT TO SAY!

THEN...

ALL RIGHT, I **HEAR YOU!** I GUESS IT'S **TRUE**--I HAVE BEEN **HEDGING MY BETS** ON THE TWO SYSTEMS...

...AND MAYBE WE ALL HAVE! BUT NOW THAT WE'VE **SURFACED** THE ISSUE IN THIS WAY, I THINK THE ONLY THING TO DO IS TO **ADD IT TO OUR AGENDA** IMMEDIATELY AND MAKE A **FINAL DECISION!**

OKAY, LET'S DO IT!

WELL, FOLKS, I THINK WE SHOULD GO FOR THE **SUPER BATTERY!**

I **AGREE!** WE'VE GOT THE **RESOURCES,** THE **TALENT** AND THE **KNOW-HOW!**

THE DEBATE GREW QUITE INTENSE AT TIMES...

BUT THIS IS A **HUGE GAMBLE!** WHAT IF WE'RE **WRONG?**

JACK, IT'S **NOT** SUCH A GAMBLE. ALL OF US IN ENGINEERING FEEL IT'S **REALLY ACHIEVABLE!**

...BUT IN THE END A **CONSENSUS** CLEARLY EMERGED!

I **TRUST** OUR ENGINEERS! IF THEY SAY THEY CAN DO IT, LET'S **BACK THEM UP!**

YOU'RE **RIGHT,** TONY! *LET'S GO FOR IT!"*

MYRNA, WHO WAS STILL **MEETING MANAGER**, BROUGHT THIS PART OF OUR DISCUSSION TO ITS **CONCLUSION!**

FRIENDS, WE SEEM TO BE IN **AGREEMENT** HERE! IS THERE ANYONE WHO DOES **NOT** FEEL ABLE TO SUPPORT OUR **FULL COMMITMENT** TO THE **SUPER BATTERY?**

WE'RE ALL AGREED!

YEP, WE SHOULD GET OFF THE FENCE!

I'M IN FAVOR OF IT!

AND SO IT WAS **AGREED!** EVERYONE **SPONTANEOUSLY** APPLAUDED! THEN WANDA HART **CAPPED** THE MOMENT WITH A STARTLING **NEW PROPOSAL...!**

I THINK WE ALL **REALIZE** WHAT AN IMPORTANT MOMENT THIS IS FOR US. IT'S ALSO A **MAGNIFICENT** OPPORTUNITY!

BECAUSE IF WE **CAN** BUILD THE **SUPER BATTERY**, WE'LL BECOME THE **TOP COMPANY** IN THE FIELD... NEVER MIND G.M.! SO I PROPOSE THAT WE PUT BECOMING **PREEMINENT** RIGHT UP FRONT IN OUR **VISION!**

EVERYONE WAS **STUNNED** BY THE **BOLDNESS** OF WANDA'S IDEA...EXCEPT **ME!** I WAS **DELIGHTED.** SLOWLY I GOT TO MY FEET, DETERMINED TO SOMEHOW **OVERCOME** THE GROUP'S **RESISTANCE!**

WANDA'S **RIGHT**...! HISTORIC MOMENT...**PREEMINENT** COMPANY...**LET'S** GO FOR IT!

YEAH!

CLAP! CLAP!

WE CAN DO IT!

I LEARNED THAT ACHIEVING **CONSEN-SUS** ISN'T **ALWAYS EASY!** IT TOOK SOME **ARGUING,** BUT BY THE TIME WE WERE DONE, THE **WHOLE GROUP** WAS **WITH** WANDA AND ME! THEN **DON BASKIN** SPOKE UP.

HARRY, I'M **PLEASED** WE'RE SO ALIGNED ABOUT **WHERE WE'RE GOING**, BUT I FEEL WE ALSO NEED TO **AGREE** ABOUT HOW TO **GET THERE!**

A **GREAT VISION** LIKE OURS **SHOULD INCLUDE** THE WAYS WE PLAN TO **DEAL WITH EACH OTHER** ON A DAILY BASIS! RIGHT NOW, THERE'S **NOT ENOUGH COOPERATION** BETWEEN **GROUPS** OR **INDIVIDUALS!**

YOU'VE GOT A **POINT**, DON! WE'VE OFTEN DISPLAYED A **SILO MENTALITY**, WITH EACH DEPARTMENT LOOKING OUT ONLY FOR **ITSELF!**

WELL, THEN, LET'S **WRITE** INTO OUR **VISION** THAT WE'LL ALL **PLAY WIN-WIN** WITH EACH OTHER!

DEIRDRE ADDED A VITAL ELEMENT!

PLAYING **WIN-WIN** MEANS ACTIVELY SEEKING **POSITIVE OUTCOMES** FOR ALL SIDES! **WIN-LOSE** BEHAVIOR INEVITABLY LEADS TO **LOSE-LOSE!** THE ONLY WAY **ANYONE** CAN WIN IS WHEN **EVERYONE WINS!**

OUR VISION
1. TOP E.V. BATTERY CO.
2. WIN-WIN BEHAVIORS

-59-

AN OPENNESS TO LEARNING!
A CUSTOMER-FIRST ETHIC!
HIGH QUALITY, LOW COST!
OTHER PIECES WERE QUICKLY ADDED...!
RAPID ADAPTATION!

AND DON BASKIN CAME UP WITH A UNIFYING FORMULA!
I LIKE IT!
YEAH!
WE CAN PULL ALL THESE IDEAS TOGETHER IF WE THINK OF OURSELVES AS A CHAIN OF INTERNAL SUPPLIERS AND CUSTOMERS! WE EACH SUPPLY AND ARE SUPPLIED! NO MORE SILOS OR BARRICADES! JUST TRUE QUALITY AND SERVICE!
GREAT IDEA, DON!
GOOD!

JOE'S ADVICE WAS THAT WE **PHRASE** OUR *VISION* IN THE **PRESENT TENSE**, AND USE **SHORT, DIRECT LANGUAGE.** IT TOOK SOME WORK, BUT EVENTUALLY WE **GOT IT!**

AFTER IT WAS POSTED, EVERYBODY **SIGNED ON!** WE HAD *OWNERSHIP!*

WE **TITLED** OUR VISION *VROOM!* IT SEEMED APPROPRIATE FOR **TONY**, WHO'D FIRST USED THE WORD, TO PRESENT THE **FINAL VERSION** TO THE GROUP!

VROOM!

Electromotion is the leading company in its field. We produce the highest-quality, lowest-cost EV batteries for our chosen markets.

We achieve our results through rapid adaptation, teamwork and a customer-first ethic.

One hundred percent responsibility, an openness to learning and win-win behaviors are the hall-marks of our culture.

Harry S. Black   Wanda Hart   Deirdre Bank   Don Baskin   Myrna Cooke   Jack Smits   Melvin Goot   Jed Roth   Brenda Frost   Mary Barton   Leslie Weiner   Daniel G. Mann   Geraldine Trent   STEVE ELVEN   Sally Jones   Tony Mills   Howard Rosenberg

THE FINAL PART OF JOE'S MEETING MANAGEMENT SYSTEM CALLED FOR THE GROUP TO SELF-EVALUATE ITS PERFORMANCE AND MAKE CORRECTIONS FOR THE FUTURE.

I THINK WE DID GREAT!

MORE PEOPLE SHOULD HAVE SPOKEN UP!

LISTENING CHECKS HELP WHEN FOLKS DISAGREE!

MAYBE I COULD BE MORE CONCISE!

I COULDN'T HAVE BEEN **MORE PLEASED!** WE HAD A **GREAT VISION** WHICH THE **WHOLE** GROUP HAD **CREATED AND ACCEPTED...**

AND IN THE **ACTION-PLUS** MEETING METHOD WE POSSESSED A **PROCESS** THAT DREW US ALL **TOGETHER** AS A **TEAM** EACH TIME WE USED IT!

EVERYONE HAD WORKED **HARD** AND **WELL** ALL DAY, AND DESERVED A GOOD, RELAXING **BREAK!** NOW I SAW THE GREAT **WISDOM** OF JOE'S RECOMMENDATION THAT WE HOLD OUR MEETING SOMEWHERE NICE! MOST OF US HEADED DIRECTLY FOR THE **BEACH!**

UNDER THE HOOD WITH HARRY

WHAT IS A VISION?

▼ A VISION DESCRIBES A PREFERRED FUTURE
AND AN ORGANIZATION'S VALUES.

WHY IS VISION IMPORTANT?

▼ A VISION LENDS PURPOSE TO ACTION
AND PROVIDES MEANING TO INDIVIDUALS.
IT ENABLES ORGANIZATIONS TO BE PROACTIVE.

HOW IS VISION ACCOMPLISHED AND MAINTAINED?

▼ THROUGH OPEN COMMUNICATION,
TRUST AND RESPECT FOR THE IDEAS
OF EACH INDIVIDUAL.
BY BEING EXPECTED AND ENCOURAGED AT ALL LEVELS.
THROUGH COMMON LANGUAGE, VALUES AND EXPERIENCES.

WHO'S RESPONSIBLE?

▼ EACH PERSON.
IT EMERGES FROM GOOD LEADERSHIP.

CHAPTER SIX
LIGHTBULBS!

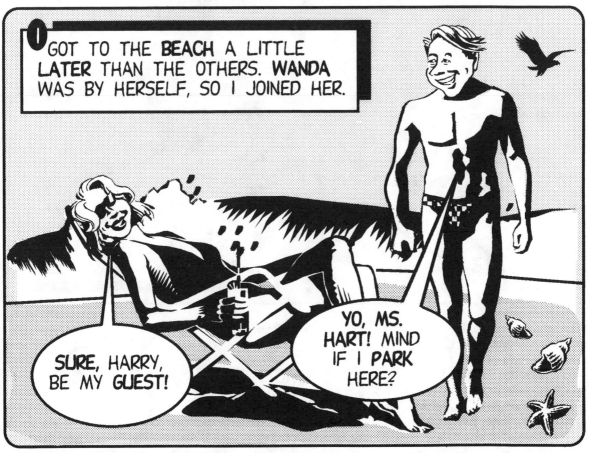

I THOUGHT OVER WANDA'S REMARK WHILE SHE FINISHED HER SWIM.

SHE'S RIGHT! JENNY AND I HAVE LOST OUR VISION...COMPETING OBJECTIVES...NO TEAMWORK... HA! I WONDER WHAT JOE WISE WOULD DO...?

AND THAT'S WHEN THE FIRST LIGHT-BULB CLICKED ON FOR ME!

I'D BEEN TRYING TO MANAGE MY MARRIAGE JUST LIKE ELECTRO-MOTION...AND WITH THE SAME LACK OF SUCCESS!

I SLEPT **BADLY** FOR A **SECOND** NIGHT, AND DREAMED MY WIFE WAS LEADING **SIX OF** ME THROUGH A **TEAM-BUILDING** EXERCISE!

AFTER BREAKFAST I **CALLED** JENNY AT HER NIECE'S HOUSE. SHE TOOK HER **TIME** COMING TO THE PHONE.

AFTER SOME **HESITATION,** JENNY **AGREED** TO COME! I HEAVED A SIGH OF **RELIEF!**

-66-

SECOND, OUR **PAY STRUCTURE** NEEDS RETHINKING! **FUNCTIONAL** GOALS HAVE BECOME PARAMOUNT BECAUSE WHAT GETS **MEASURED** AND **REWARDED** IS WHAT GETS **DONE**. THIS HAS LED TO THE 'SILO MENTALITY' OF MYOPIC **DEPARTMENTAL AGENDAS**, CREATING MISTAKES, DELAYS, REWORK, SCRAP, AND **LOST OPPORTUNITIES!**

OBSTACL
POW
* PAY
* PROC

AND **FINALLY,** WE THINK ELECTRO'S ENTIRE **R&D** PROCESS SHOULD BE **RE-EXAMINED** AND **REVAMPED.** THE PROBLEMS I'VE OUTLINED ARE **INHERENT** IN OUR **CURRENT** SYSTEM! IF DEVELOPING THE SUPER BATTERY IS INDEED OUR **CHIEF PRIORITY**, THEN WE NEED TO REORGANIZE AROUND IT **FULLY! ONWARD** AND **UPWARD,** FRIENDS!

OBSTACLES
* POWER
* PAY
* PROCESS

IT WAS A **GREAT SPEECH,** A **TURNING POINT** IN THE HISTORY OF ELECTROMOTION!

THANK YOU, THANK YOU!

EXCELLENT!

LET'S GIVE HIM A CLAP, FOLKS!

I SENSED THAT THE MOMENT WAS **RIGHT** TO MOVE ON TO THE **NEXT PHASE** OF JOE'S *TCTB PROCESS!*

FOLKS, PLEASE **NOTICE** THAT WHAT WE'RE **DOING** RIGHT NOW IS GIVING OUR VISION THE **CONTOURS OF REALITY!** THAT'S A GREAT STEP **FORWARD!**

YESTERDAY, WHEN WE BEGAN OUR CLIMB TOWARDS **GREATNESS**, WE AGREED THAT AFTER **AFFIRMING OUR VISION** WE'D DECIDE WHERE TO BUILD OUR **BASE CAMPS.** I CALLED THESE CAMPS OUR CSF'S...*CRITICAL SUCCESS FACTORS!*

A **CRITICAL SUCCESS FACTOR** IS A CONDITION THAT MUST **BE IN PLACE** IF OUR VISION IS TO BE **REALIZED.** IT'S SOMETHING **MEASURABLE** OR AT LEAST **OBSERVABLE,** AND ALSO ACTS AS A KIND OF **MARKER** SO THAT WE'LL KNOW WE'RE ON **TARGET** AS OUR **ASCENT** CONTINUES!

FOR EXAMPLE, OUR MOST OBVIOUS CSF IS AN EFFECTIVE AND EFFICIENT PROCESS FOR DEVELOPING THE **SUPER BATTERY!** IF WE DON'T HAVE *THAT*, WE HAVE NOTHING!

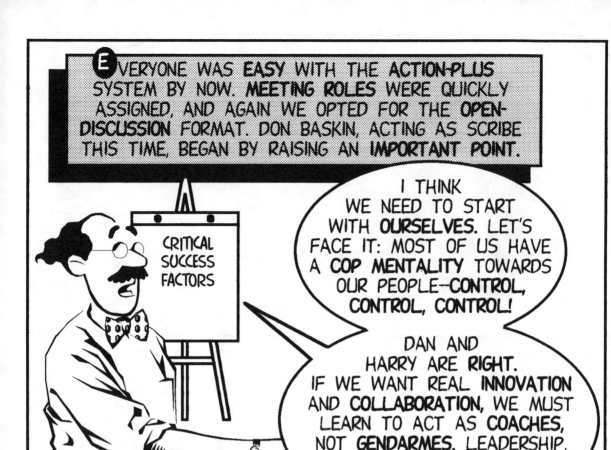

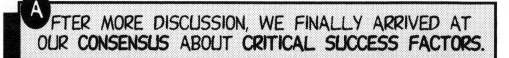

AFTER MORE DISCUSSION, WE FINALLY ARRIVED AT OUR CONSENSUS ABOUT CRITICAL SUCCESS FACTORS.

CSF 1: THE WHOLE COMPANY IS ALIGNED AROUND A COMMON PURPOSE.

CSF 2: WE HAVE AN EFFECTIVE AND EFFICIENT PROCESS TO PRODUCE THE SUPER BATTERY!

CSF 3: WE USE A TEAM APPROACH WITHIN AND ACROSS FUNCTIONS. TEAMS ARE BEING TRAINED TO SELF-MANAGE THEIR WORK.

CSF 4: MANAGERS AND SUPERVISORS ACT AS COACHES, NOT COPS!

CSF 5: FRAGMENTED TASKS ARE COMBINED. MULTIPLE SKILLS ARE REWARDED, AS WELL AS SPECIALIZED KNOW-HOW.

CSF 6: APPRAISAL AND PAY SYSTEMS REWARD TEAM RESULTS AND MVP PERFORMANCE.

CRITICAL SUCCESS FACTORS

1. COMMON PURPOSE. EVERYONE ENROLLED.

2. EFFICIENT SUPER BATTERY PROCESS.

3. CROSS-FUNCTIONAL TEAM APPROACH. TRAINING FOR SELF-MANAGEMENT.

4. MANAGERS AS COACHES, NOT COPS.

5. WHOLE JOBS. MULTIPLE SKILLS.

6. APPRAISAL & PAY SYSTEMS REWARD TEAM RESULTS & MVP PERFORMANCE.

WE'RE MAKING **GREAT PROGRESS**, FRIENDS! BUT NOW WE HAVE TO GIVE THESE CSF'S **REAL SUBSTANCE**. THE **FIRST** THING TO DO IS SET UP A **RESPONSIBILITY NETWORK**--AN INTERCONNECTED WEB OF TEAMS DEDICATED TO **ACHIEVING THEM!**

NATURALLY, THEY ALSO HAVE TO BE **PRIORITIZED** AND GIVEN **TIME LINES**, BUT WE CAN DO THAT AFTER WE GET BACK **HOME**.

THIS TIME AROUND, I'D BEEN ASKED TO ACT AS **MEETING MANAGER**. AFTER PRESENTING THE FINAL LIST OF CSF'S TO THE GROUP, I MOVED THE MEETING ON TO ITS **NEXT LEVEL!**

EACH OF OUR CRITICAL SUCCESS FACTORS NEEDS A GROUP --A TEAM--RESPONSIBLE FOR MAKING IT **HAPPEN!** AT THE SAME TIME, EACH TEAM HAS TO **KNOW** WHAT'S **GOING ON** ELSEWHERE, SO DEVELOPMENTS CAN BE **COORDINATED** AND PLANNED!

THAT'S WHERE THE **NETWORK** COMES IN!

1. Enrolling Others	2. Super Battery Process	3. Self-Mgng. Teams	4. Mgt. Training	Whole Jobs.	6. Pay, etc.
Goal Champion	Goal Champion				Goal Champion
Expert	E				
Support					
Support	Supp				port
Support	Support	Support	Support	Support	Support

MEMBERSHIP OF EACH TEAM IS VOLUNTARY, AND PEOPLE **NOMINATE THEMSELVES!**

TEAM LEADERS ARE ELECTED, AND KNOWN AS *GOAL CHAMPIONS.* THEY CO-ORDINATE THEIR GROUP'S WORK AND TAKE **OVERALL RESPONSIBILITY** FOR ITS SUCCESS!

OTHER TEAM MEMBERS FUNCTION AS EITHER *EXPERTS* OR *SUPPORTS.* **EXPERTS** PROVIDE SPECIALIZED KNOWLEDGE OR INFORMATION.

SUPPORT PEOPLE AGREE TO DO WHAT-EVER ADDITIONAL **TASKS** ARE **NECESSARY** TO MAKE THE CSF A **REALITY!**

UNDER THE HOOD WITH HARRY

CREATING A DESIRED FUTURE

SUPPORTIVE CULTURE

CUSTOMER-ORIENTED SYSTEMS, STRUCTURES & PROCESSES

ALIGNMENT/ COMMON PURPOSE

VISION OF DESIRED FUTURE

TEAMWORK/ COACHING

STRATEGY & PLANNNING

INSPIRED PERFORMANCE IS NO ACCIDENT.
OUTSTANDING RESULTS BECOME POSSIBLE WHEN AN
ORGANIZATION IS ALIGNED AROUND A VISION OF A DESIRED FUTURE,
AND DESIGNS AND INSTITUTES SUPPORTIVE AND SYNERGISTIC HUMAN
AND TECHNICAL STRUCTURES AND SYSTEMS.

CHAPTER SEVEN
HARRY SETS THE STAGE

MR. BLACK, TELEPHONE!

WAS JUST GETTING MY LUNCH WHEN THERE WAS A PHONE CALL FOR ME!

TO MY SURPRISE AND DELIGHT, IT WAS JOE WISE!

SO, HARRY, HOW'S IT GOING?

FANTASTIC, JOE! THIS TURBO-CHARGED TEAM-BUILDING METHOD OF YOURS IS JUST INCREDIBLE!

SO FAR WE'VE CREATED A VISION, IDENTIFIED SIX CRITICAL SUCCESS FACTORS, AND DEVELOPED A RESPONSIBILITY MATRIX TO IMPLEMENT THEM!

JOE ASKED ME TO **READ** OUR **VISION** TO HIM, AND THEN DESCRIBE THE **CRITICAL SUCCESS FACTORS** WE'D LISTED. I COULD HEAR HIM **GRUNT** WITH APPROVAL.

HMM! YOU'VE ALL DONE **VERY WELL,** HARRY. YOUR GROUP'S EXACTLY WHERE IT **SHOULD** BE AT THIS STAGE!

BUT NOW COMES THE **HARD PART!** WHAT YOU DO NEXT CAN *MAKE OR BREAK EVERYTHING!*

IT'S TIME TO BRING YOUR TEAM MEMBERS TOGETHER --TO **WELD** THEM INTO A **HIGH-PERFORMING UNIT** CAPABLE OF SWIFT, CREATIVE INITIATIVES, **HIGH TRUST** AND INTELLIGENT **DECISION-MAKING!**

AND THAT MEANS ULTIMATELY **CLEANING UP** YOUR PAST AND EXISTING **RELATIONSHIPS,** THEN LAYING THE GROUNDWORK FOR YOUR **FUTURE INTERACTIONS** TOGETHER!

THIS AFTERNOON'S SESSION, HARRY, IS GOING TO **TEST** YOUR **GRASP** OF THE *TCTB METHOD* TO THE FULL!

"YOU BETTER **BELIEVE** THE **LONG HAIR**, TONY! AND FOR A **WHILE THERE** THE FOUR OF US WERE DOING **GOOD**!

"WE HAD OUR **OWN STYLE** AND EVEN STARTED WRITING OUR OWN MUSIC! **YOURS TRULY** HAD A STARRING NUMBER CALLED *LADY NOSTRADAMUS*!

"WE WERE GETTING **GIGS** ALL THE TIME, AND **CBS RECORDS** WERE TALKING ABOUT **AUDITIONING** US!

"AND THEN, **JUST** AS WE WERE ON THE **VERGE** OF SUCCESS, OUR GROUP **FELL APART**! IN ABOUT A WEEK WE **LOST EVERYTHING** WE'D STRUGGLED FOR OVER FIVE OR SIX **YEARS** OF HARD, HARD **WORK**!"

LAY-DEE NOSTRADAMUS, I LOVE YEW...!

"ONE EVENING WE HAD A **HUGE BLOW-OUT** IN WHICH EVERYONE FINALLY OPENED THEIR **HEARTS** AND **ALL** THE PAIN **OOZED** OUT.

"BY THE TIME WE WERE **DONE**, IT WAS OBVIOUS THERE WAS **NO WAY** OUR BAND COULD **CONTINUE!**

"AND SO I BECAME AN **ENGINEER!**"

HARRY, **WHAT** YOU SEEM TO BE **SAYING** IS THAT IF WE WANT TO **HOLD TOGETHER** AS A **TEAM**, WE NEED SOME WAY TO **DEFUSE** TENSIONS AND CONFLICTS WHEN THEY **ARISE!**

YOU'RE **RIGHT**, SALLY! PEOPLE WORKING TOGETHER INEVITABLY **CHAFE** AND **RUB**! SO IF WE'RE TO SUCCEED AS A TEAM, WE MUST AGREE ON A **MECHANISM** TO **DEAL** WITH IT— OR WE'LL **FOLD** JUST LIKE MY **BAND!**

BUT **BEFORE** WE GO FURTHER, WE SHOULD FIRST **CLEAR UP** ANY **HANGOVER** ISSUES FROM THE **PAST**, SO THAT WE CAN ALL **START** WITH A **CLEAN SLATE!**

UNDER THE HOOD WITH HARRY

LEADING BY EXAMPLE

IN CHAPTER SEVEN, HARRY DEMONSTRATES LEADERSHIP BY
ANTEING UP FIRST AND MODELING NEW BEHAVIORS.

HARRY PUTS INTO PRACTICE THE PREMISE:

"YOU CAN ONLY LEAD OTHERS
WHERE YOU YOURSELF ARE WILLING TO GO."

CHAPTER EIGHT

THE FEEDBACK SESSION

IT TURNS OUT THAT IN **ORGANIZATIONS** THERE ARE TWO WAYS TO **INCREASE** THE **AREA** OF **SHARED** KNOWLEDGE AND INTEREST: **SELF-DISCLOSURE** AND GIVING/RECEIVING **FEEDBACK!**

SELF-DISCLOSURE IS WHAT WE CHOOSE TO TELL **OTHERS** ABOUT **OURSELVES.**

FEEDBACK IS WHAT **THEY** TELL **US** ABOUT THE EFFECT OF OUR BEHAVIORS ON **THEM!**

THE **BEST** AND MOST **FAMOUS** **ILLUSTRATION** OF THESE IDEAS IS THE **JOHARI WINDOW,** NAMED AFTER ITS CREATORS, **JOSEPH LUFT** AND **HARRY INGHAM.**

THE **WINDOW** IS A WAY OF **DESCRIBING** HOW WE **GIVE** AND **RECEIVE** INFORMATION ABOUT **OURSELVES** AND **OTHERS.**

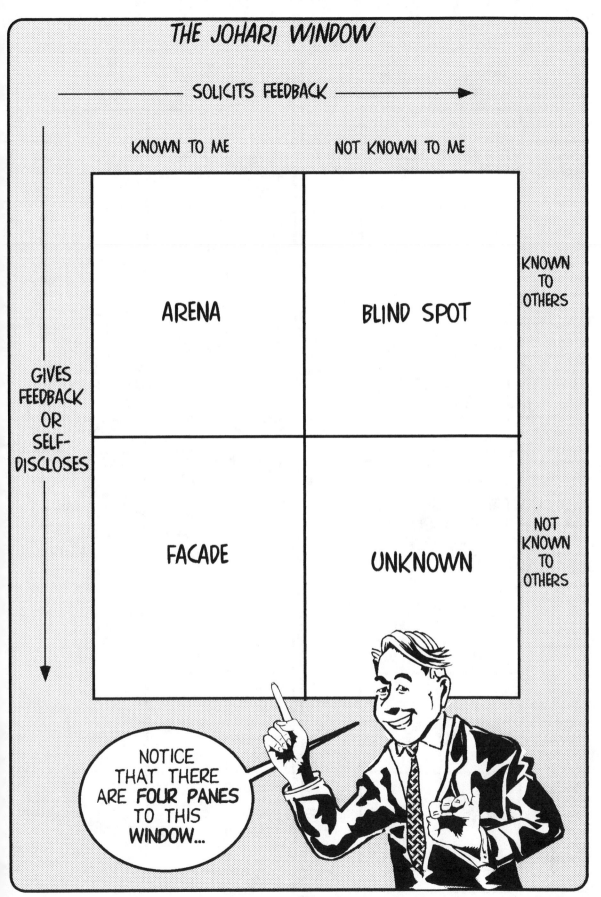

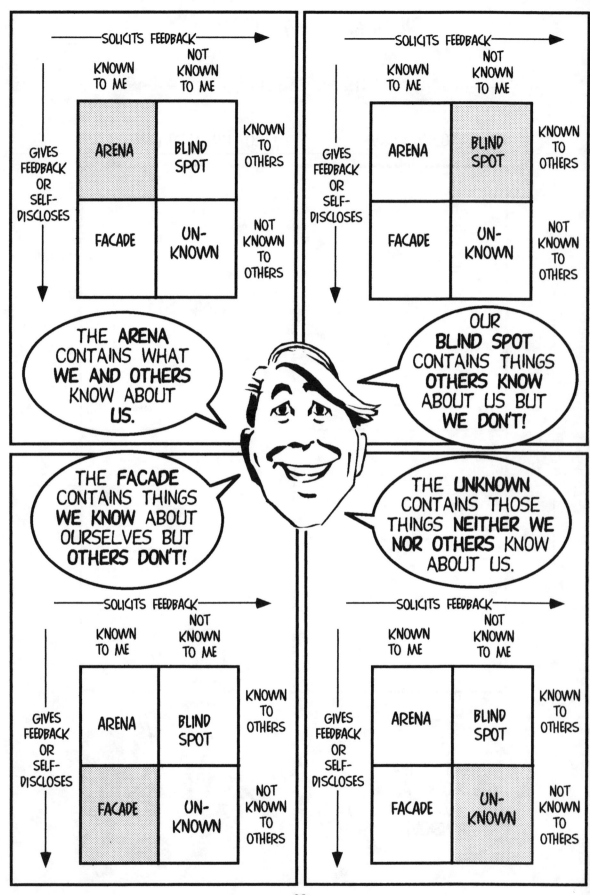

HARRY, THIS IS **REALLY** INTERESTING, BUT IT HAS SERIOUS IMPLICATIONS!

WHEN YOU SAY **SELF-DISCLOSE**, YOU MEAN I HAVE TO **MOVE** INFORMATION ABOUT **MYSELF** FROM MY **FACADE** INTO THE PUBLIC **ARENA**!

AND, **FRANKLY,** I'M **NOT SURE** I WANT TO **DO** THAT!

I MEAN, MAYBE THAT'S THE REASON I HAVE A **FACADE** IN THE FIRST PLACE!

YOU'RE **RIGHT,** DAN! BUT THAT'S WHY WE USE THE TERM **APPROPRIATE** SELF-DISCLOSURE! NO ONE'S TALKING ABOUT **TRUE CONFESSIONS** HERE!

ALL WE'RE LOOKING TO DO IS **SHARE THINGS** ABOUT OURSELVES THAT ARE **RELEVANT**--FOR EXAMPLE, CORE **VALUES,** PAST **EXPERIENCES** WITH THE JOB, AND SO ON!

SINCERELY DONE, IT HELPS BUILD **TRUST,** CONFIDENCE IN YOUR **LEADERSHIP** AND TEAM **SOLIDARITY!**

ACTUALLY, SELF-DISCLOSING IS OFTEN **EASIER** THAN THE **SECOND LEG** OF THIS WALK-- GIVING AND RECEIVING FEEDBACK!

LIKE SELF-DISCLOSURE, **USEFUL FEEDBACK** FOLLOWS CERTAIN **PRINCIPLES**. ITS **PURPOSE** IS TO **HELP** RECEIVERS BECOME **AWARE** OF THE **IMPACT** OF THEIR BE- HAVIORS ON OTHERS. INFORMATION IS MOVED FROM THE RECEIVER'S **BLIND SPOT** INTO THE **ARENA!**

FOR THIS REASON, THE **FIRST PRINCIPLE OF FEEDBACK** IS THAT THE RECEIVER MUST BE **WILLING** AND **READY** TO **HEAR** IT!

SECONDLY, **GIVERS** MUST BE CERTAIN THAT THEIR **INTENTIONS** ARE TO BE **TRULY** HELPFUL. THERE'S **NO ROOM** HERE FOR **POINT-SCORING** OR CRITICISM DESIGNED SIMPLY TO MAKE **THEM** LOOK OR FEEL **BETTER!**

THIRD, FEEDBACK SHOULD DEAL WITH **SPECIFIC BEHAVIORS** RECEIVERS CAN ACTUALLY **DO** SOME- THING ABOUT! TELLING SOMEONE THEY'RE **TOO SHORT** DOESN'T HELP!

FINALLY, GIVE FEEDBACK AS **SOON** AS POSSIBLE **AFTER** THE BEHAVIOR YOU'RE REACTING TO.

MY FIRST BIG **SURPRISE** WAS HOW MANY WRITTEN, **ANONYMOUS** COMMENTS I GOT!

AND MY **SECOND** WAS HOW MANY SAID MORE OR LESS THE **SAME THING!**

Harry, At our monthly meetings you often say that it's better to ask for forgiveness than for permission, but when things don't go the way you'd like, you get angry!

Harry

You tell us it's OK to take risks, but often blow up when things go wrong. The message is "don't screw up." Do you really want a new culture here, or a CYA culture?

TOUGH AS IT IS, FOLKS, I WANT TO **THANK** YOU! LIKE THEY SAY, WHEN **ONE** PERSON TELLS YOU YOU'RE A **HORSE,** WELL, MAYBE THAT'S JUST HIS **OPINION.** WHEN **TWO** PEOPLE DO, IT'S A **POSSIBILITY!** BUT WHEN **THREE, FOUR, FIVE** SAY SO—YOU'D BETTER GET YOURSELF A **SADDLE!**

FRIENDS, GETTING YOUR **FEEDBACK** LIKE THIS HAS BEEN A REALLY **POSITIVE** EXPERIENCE FOR ME--DIFFICULT BUT POSITIVE!

AND NOW IT'S **YOUR TURN!** IN A MOMENT I'M GOING TO ASK **EACH** OF YOU TO MEET **PRIVATELY, IN PAIRS,** WITH THOSE PEOPLE YOU'D LIKE TO **GIVE--** AND **GET--**SOME **FEEDBACK** FROM!

ASKING FOR FEEDBACK THE **RIGHT WAY** IS JUST AS **IMPORTANT** AS **GIVING** IT! FOLLOW THESE GUIDELINES.

1. SPECIFY THOSE BEHAVIORS YOU WANT FEEDBACK ABOUT.

2. RESTATE GIVER'S COMMENTS TO MAKE SURE YOU UNDERSTAND.

3. DON'T ACT DEFENSIVELY!

4. SHARE WHAT YOU MIGHT DO ABOUT NEGATIVE FEEDBACK.

KEEP IN MIND THAT MOST **COMPLAINTS** ARE IMPLICIT **REQUESTS** FOR **BEHAVIORAL CHANGE.** HERE ARE **FOUR** WAYS YOU CAN ANSWER: *I'LL DO IT; NO, AND HERE'S WHY; I'LL DO IT UNDER THESE CONDITIONS; I NEED TO THINK ABOUT IT AND GET BACK TO YOU...*

UNDER THE HOOD WITH HARRY

TRUST AND TEAMWORK

INSPIRED PERFORMING TEAMWORK REQUIRES A HIGH
LEVEL OF TRUST BETWEEN TEAM MEMBERS.

KEY ELEMENTS OF TRUST BUILDING:

1. CONSISTENTLY MEETING COMMITMENTS AND KEEPING
AGREEMENTS FOSTERS A SENSE OF YOUR INTEGRITY.
(SEE GROUND RULES IN CHAPTER 9.)

2. ANTEING UP FIRST. DISCLOSING TO OTHERS WHAT
YOU STAND FOR, ENCOURAGES THEM TO TAKE THE
RISK OF BEING OPEN WITH YOU, A KEY STEP
IN BUILDING TRUST.
(SEE HARRY'S EXAMPLES IN CHAPTERS 7 AND 8.)

3. LISTENING CAREFULLY AND GENUINELY TRYING
TO UNDERSTAND OTHERS' POINTS OF VIEW
DEMONSTRATES YOUR RESPECT AND CARING,
WHICH FOSTERS TRUST.

4. BEING OPEN ABOUT YOUR ACTIONS AND
INTENTIONS AND AVOIDING SECRECY REDUCE
THREAT AND ORGANIZATIONAL POLITICS, WHICH
INEVITABLY UNDERMINE TRUST.

CHAPTER NINE
GROUND RULES

WHAT DO YOU MEAN, **BASIC RULES**, HARRY? LIKE THE **TEN COMMANDMENTS** OR SOMETHING?

NO, DAN, NOT EXACTLY...!

"OVER **TIME**, ALL GROUPS DEVELOP **BEHAVIORAL HABITS.** SOME OF THEM **HELP THEIR PURPOSE**, OTHERS **HINDER** IT! IN **ORGANIZATIONS**, HABITS LIKE THESE FUNCTION AS **UNSPOKEN RULES** THAT ARE OFTEN FAR MORE **POWERFUL** THAN THE OFFICIAL, SO-CALLED **SPOKEN RULES** TO WHICH EVERYONE PAYS **LIP SERVICE!**"

ELECTROMOTION'S GROUND RULES

1. I MAKE ONLY CLEAR AGREEMENTS AND PLANS I INTEND TO KEEP.
2. WHEN AN AGREEMENT MUST BE BROKEN, I NOTIFY A.S.A.P.
3. IF I BREAK AN AGREEMENT, I QUICKLY RECONCILE WITH THE AFFECTED PERSON.
4. I AM 100 PERCENT RESPONSIBLE, AND I CAN'T DO IT ALONE.
5. I AM HONEST AND OPEN IN ALL MY DEALINGS.
6. WHEN AN ISSUE ARISES, I INTERACT PROMPTLY AND DIRECTLY WITH THE PERSON CONCERNED.
7. I EMPHASIZE LISTENING MORE THAN SPEAKING.
8. I DO NOT CRITICIZE WITHOUT VOICING AN ALTERNATIVE.
9. I FOCUS ON DESIRED RESULTS, AND PLAY WIN-WIN AT ALL TIMES.
10. ONCE A DECISION IS MADE, I SUPPORT IT 100 PERCENT.

I STILL KEEP A **COPY** OF THOSE **HISTORIC** GROUND RULES **MOUNTED** AND **FRAMED** IN MY OFFICE!

AFTER THE SESSION **ENDED**, I WENT FOR ANOTHER **SOLO** WALK ALONG THE BEACH. **THRILLED** AND **EXALTED**, I COULD ALMOST **PHYSICALLY** SENSE MY **TEAM** COMING TOGETHER! AND **JENNY** WOULD **SOON** BE WITH ME, TOO! I HEADED **BACK** TO THE HOTEL, **RELISHING** THOUGHTS OF THE FINAL **DAY!**

UNDER THE HOOD WITH HARRY

TEAM GROUND RULES

GROUND RULES DESCRIBE SPECIFIC DAY-TO-DAY BEHAVIORS AND ATTITUDES THAT EACH PERSON WILL ADOPT IN SERVICE OF THE TEAM'S VISION.

IN ADDITION TO ELECTROMOTION'S GROUND RULES, GIVEN ON PAGE 123, HERE ARE SOME OTHER EXAMPLES THAT MAY BE HELPFUL TO YOUR TEAM:

 I ACCEPT AND SUPPORT OUR VISION, OPERATING OBJECTIVES AND GROUND RULES.

 I WILL OPERATE PUNCTUALLY.

 I WILL ACCENTUATE THE POSITIVE AND VIEW PROBLEMS AS OPPORTUNITIES.

 I WILL NOT AGREE UNLESS I BELIEVE (E.G., NOT JUST TO PLEASE THE BOSS).

 I WILL WORK TO ACHIEVE SUCCESS FOR EVERYONE IN THE COMPANY.

 I MEAN EVERYTHING I SAY, AND I WILL NOT SPEAK TO MISLEAD.

CHAPTER TEN
ROLLING OUT THE VISION

THE MORNING OF THE LAST DAY...

WELCOME, FOLKS, TO OUR FINAL SESSION.

ROLLING OUT THE VISION

AS YOU **KNOW**, WE'RE SCHEDULED TO **END** BY **NOON**, AND WE STILL HAVE SOME **CRUCIAL** BUSINESS TO ATTEND TO!

WE'VE LAID THE **FOUNDATION** FOR OUR OWN **UNITY** AND **COMMITMENT**. NOW WE NEED TO THINK ABOUT **BRINGING THE WORD** TO THE **REST** OF ELECTRO-MOTION.

I CALL THIS PROCESS *ROLLING OUT THE VISION!*

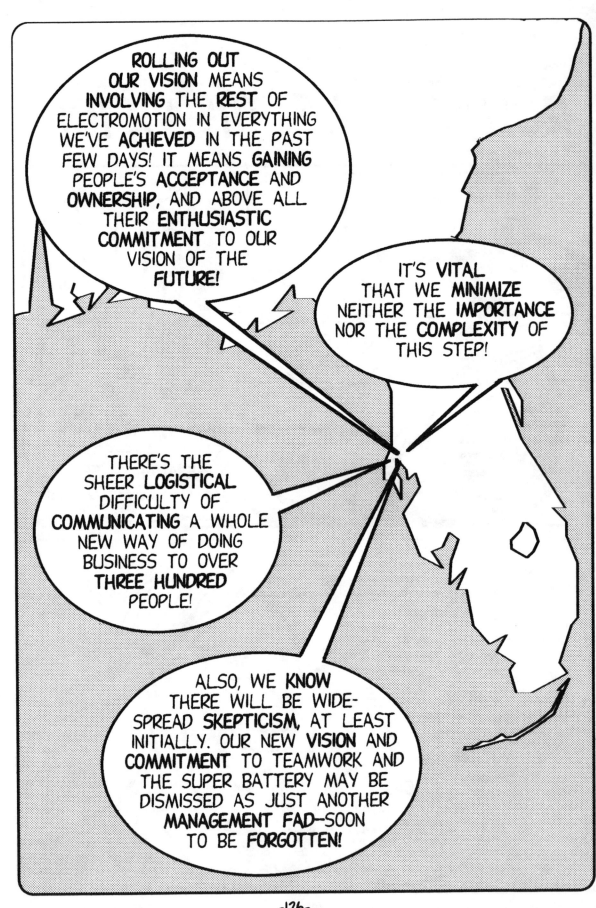

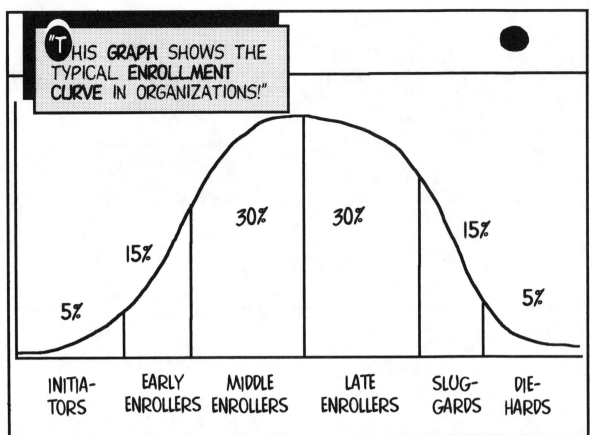

THE VERY **UNIQUENESS** OF THE OCCASION WILL **DEMONSTRATE** TO EVERYONE THAT WE REALLY **MEAN BUSINESS!** I INTEND TO SPEAK TO THE **ENTIRE COMPANY,** TELLING THEM THAT I'M **OFF THE FENCE** ABOUT THE **HYBRID** VERSUS THE **SUPER BATTERY...**AND ASK FOR THEIR HELP AND COOPERATION!

I **AGREE** WITH HARRY. WE CAN PULL OFF A BIG MEETING WITH **GOOD PLANNING.** I VOLUNTEER TO LEAD THE **ORGANIZING TEAM!**

I WAS **ESPECIALLY** GLAD TO GET SALLY'S SUPPORT AT THIS POINT! WE REALLY **HAD** CLEANED UP THINGS BETWEEN US IN THE **FEEDBACK SESSION!**

THANKS, SALLY!

YEAH, HARRY!

OKAY, LET'S GO FOR IT!

FOLKS, DO WE HAVE **CONSENSUS** AROUND DEIRDRE'S SUGGESTION?

ONE BY ONE PEOPLE CAME **FORWARD** TO **DECLARE** THEMSELVES. THERE WERE **NO** HANGOVER ISSUES--EVERYONE WAS **UPBEAT** AND **POSITIVE!**

FRIENDS, I MUST **ADMIT** I WAS **SKEPTICAL** AT FIRST, BUT YOU'VE MADE A **BELIEVER** OUT OF ME! LET'S **VROOM!**

AND WE'VE **APPRECIATED** YOUR PROFESSIONALISM, DAN!

ALSO YOUR WILLINGNESS TO KEEP AN **OPEN MIND!**

DAN, **THANKS** FOR THE **FEEDBACK** YOU GAVE ME!

SALLY, **THANKS** FOR **FOCUSING** US ON THE **SUPER BATTERY!**

YOU HAD THE **COURAGE** TO TAKE AN **INITIATIVE** AT THE RIGHT TIME!

I REALLY **APPRECIATED** YOUR **SINCERITY!**

I'M SO **PLEASED** ABOUT OUR **COMMITMENT** TO THE **SUPER BATTERY!** AS HEAD ENGINEER, I **PLEDGE** MYSELF **100 PERCENT** BEHIND THE NEW APPROACH!

FOLKS, SOMETHING **SPECIAL** HAS HAPPENED HERE! I'M **PROUD** TO BE PART OF IT!

WE'RE **PROUD** OF YOU, DEIRDRE!

YOU HAVE **GROWN** IN THE PAST **THREE DAYS!**

YES, YOU EMERGED AS A **LEADER!**

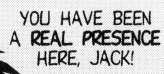

I'M EXCITED AT THE PROSPECT OF **REAL CULTURE** CHANGE! **TEAMS** ARE THE WAVE OF THE FUTURE IN **BUSINESS**! I'LL BE **WORKING HARD** FOR OUR **SUCCESS**!

YOU HAVE BEEN A **REAL PRESENCE** HERE, JACK!

I REMEMBER, YOU WERE THE **FIRST** ONE TO USE THE WORD **"CHANGE!"**

AND YOU SHOWED REAL **MVP** TEAM PLAY!

TONY, YOUR **ABILITY** TO MAKE PEOPLE FEEL **ACCEPTED** WAS A BIG **PLUS**!

YOUR **HUMOR**! I **LOVE** IT!

I **ADMIRE** YOUR COMMITMENT TO **ELECTROMOTION'S SUCCESS**!

I'M **COMPLETELY** IN FAVOR OF THIS! IT HAS MY **FULL** SUPPORT!

MYRNA, YOUR **ORIGINALITY** AND **CREATIVITY** ARE TERRIFIC!

I **ADMIRE** YOUR ABILITY TO MODEL **NEW BEHAVIOR**!

I FELT ALL ALONG THAT WE COULD DO IT! LET'S GO!

AS THE PROCESS GATHERED **MOMENTUM**, I FOUND MYSELF **DEEPLY MOVED** BY OUR GROWING SENSE OF **SOLIDARITY** AND, YES, EVEN **COMRADESHIP**!

YOUR **ENTHUSIASM** LIFTS US ALL!

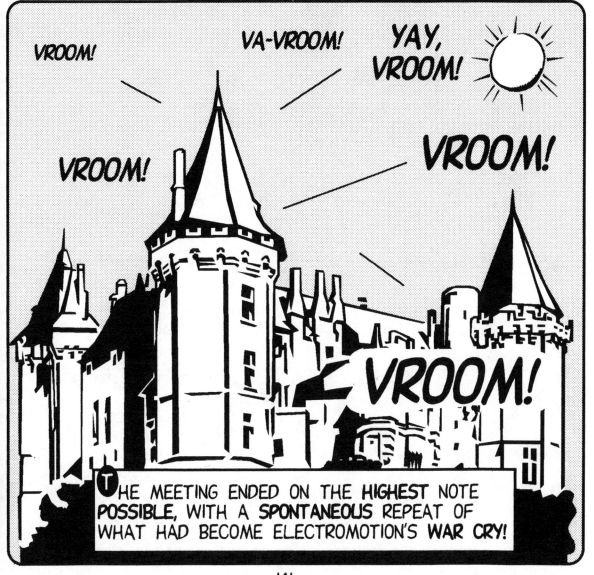

UNDER THE HOOD WITH HARRY

INVOLVING EVERYONE IN CHANGE

HARRY AND HIS TEAM ARE ALIGNED AND HAVE DECIDED TO BRING THE WHOLE OF ELECTROMOTION TOGETHER IN THE SAME PLACE AND AT THE SAME TIME TO ADDRESS THE COMPANY'S COLLECTIVE FUTURE. BEING PREPARED TO HEAR FEEDBACK AND MAKE CORRESPONDING ADJUSTMENTS TO THE DIRECTION THEY HAVE FORGED IS KEY TO SUCCESS. BENEFITS OF THIS APPROACH INCLUDE:

 UNLEASHING EXTRAORDINARY ENERGY AND COMMITMENT TO A DESIRED FUTURE.

 FOSTERING HONEST DIALOGUE ABOUT CURRENT CONDITIONS.

 CREATING PSYCHOLOGICAL OWNERSHIP OF THE CHANGE PROCESS.

 ASSOCIATING CHANGE WITH "REAL" WORK.

 SAVING TIME IN THE LONG TERM. THE PROCESS SETS THE STAGE FOR SYSTEMWIDE CHANGE TO OCCUR RAPIDLY.

CHAPTER ELEVEN

JENNY

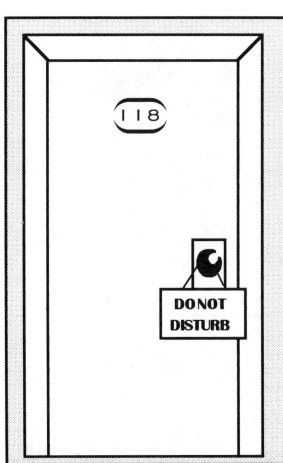

MY FRIEND, YOU **DON'T** NEED TO KNOW THE **INTIMATE** DETAILS OF JENNY'S **FEED-BACK**--OR MY **RESPONSE!** WE WENT BACK TO OUR HOTEL ROOM, AND IT'S **ENOUGH** TO SAY THAT IT TOOK US THE **WHOLE** OF THE REST OF THE **DAY** AND MOST OF THE **EVENING** TO CLEAN THINGS UP BETWEEN US--BUT WE **DID IT.** BY THE TIME WE WERE DONE, OUR **MARRIAGE** WAS ON A **SURER** FOOTING THAN EVER **BEFORE!**

EPILOGUE

FOR YOUR EASY REFERENCE, HERE ARE THE KEY CONCEPTS WITH THEIR PAGE NUMBERS.

KEY CONCEPT INDEX